T0380964

WHISPERS FROM Heaven

Lynn McKendry

To order additional copies of this book, contact:
Xlibris
1-888-795-4274
www.Xlibris.com
Orders@Xlibris.com

Foreword

My professional background is scientific in nature. I am well versed in research and the scientific method as I have two master degrees and a doctoral degree. When my Dad passed in 2010 and my Mother passed in 2012 I did not expect any supernatural occurrences. I was extremely surprised when I began to experience Whispers From Heaven. At first I was not sure what these communications were, but as I shared my stories with other people, I found that I was not alone. My experiences ranged from subtle to profound and so did other people's communication with loved ones that had died. I am convinced it is the energy of our loved ones trying to comfort us. What I have found is that usually the whispers come shortly after people die and then over time there is no more earthly communications. These stories touch my heart and I know we will someday be reunited with our loved ones in Heaven.

I am not good at end of life scenarios. I chose not to be there for my Dad's passing and the same with my Mother's end of life. I think what pushed me over the edge is when years previously my husband and I had to make the decision to euthanize our male golden retriever who had lung cancer. A colleague of mine told me to be there through the lethal injection and bitter end. Wrong decision for me. I had nightmares for months and it traumatized me like I did not expect. I think that is why I avoided the last moments with my parents, and subsequently friends that were ready to pass. Yet I have experienced communication after death in many circumstances with the people and pets that I have loved. Those communications have surprised me to no end. This is a book that chronicles some of those experiences.

(PLEASE NOTE: names of the people who have shared with me their stories are altered to protect their privacy)

My Dad, Dr. RDC

We were up at our Tahoe home for Christmas and snow skiing when my Dad called to tell me he was diagnosed with stage four metastatic cancer in his shoulder. That was in December of 2009. We didn't have much time to process things as the doctors prescribed no treatment, only hospice. He died at home in his hospital bed, surrounded by family and friends on February 9, 2010.

My Stepmom, Sandra, was the love of my Dad's life. She planned a celebration of life partly because that was what my Dad wanted. We were to have a memorial service first and Sandra asked me if I would say a few words about my Dad. We were up in Tahoe again, and planned on driving down to Nipomo for the celebration. I was not sure if I was up to speaking publicly, as I was crying daily since he died.

We were driving through the Tahoe mountains as I reminisced about my Dad's life. I went to live with him (being a child of divorce) when I was fifteen. He was a bachelor then and practiced dentistry. We lived in a beautiful home in the Palos Verdes Hills. My Dad allowed me to be a wild teenager but also taught me many things. My job after high school classes was to work in his dental office as a dental assistant. He owned an exotic sports car which he taught me how to drive. My Dad was an avid skier and loved down hill skiing. He traveled all over the world to the most beautiful ski resorts. He took me on many ski trips where he taught me how to ski. I was thinking about all these memories as I was trying to formulate what I would say at his memorial service.

I remembered the summer my Dad and Sandra came to our Tahoe home and we went to see Diana Krall perform as my Dad and I loved her music. I remembered that every spring my Dad and I would play golf together for our birthdays which were a month apart. I remembered sitting around the dining table taste-testing red wine and chocolate as my Dad tried to educate us about how well they blended together. That night my Dad told me what a wonderful life he had experienced and that there were no regrets. "When I die," he said, "don't cry for me Argentina."

These memories flooded through my mind as we drove down the mountain. A Carrie Underwood song came on the radio that I had never heard before. "Temporary Home" melody seemed to fit my mood perfectly. Then the last verse was sung:

Old man, hospital bed
The room is filled with people he loves
And he whispers
"Don't cry for me, I'll see you all some day"
He looks up and says
"I can see God's face."
This is my temporary home, it's not where I belong
Windows and rooms that I'm passing through
This was just a stop on the way to where I'm going
I'm not afraid because I know
This is my temporary home

Tears streamed down my face. I sensed my Dad's spirit and I knew the words I would speak at his memorial service.

A few days later we drove down to Nipomo. My Dad lived on a golf course and you had to travel on a long, tree-lined country road to get to his home. Suddenly, as we turned on that road "Temporary Home" came on the radio and ended precisely when we pulled into the driveway. I was crying as, again, I sensed my Dad's spirit. "What a coincidence?" I thought. But a couple of days later when we were leaving after the celebration of life, that song came on the radio precisely when we were pulling out of the driveway. These days I know it was not a coincidence. It was my Dad trying to comfort me.

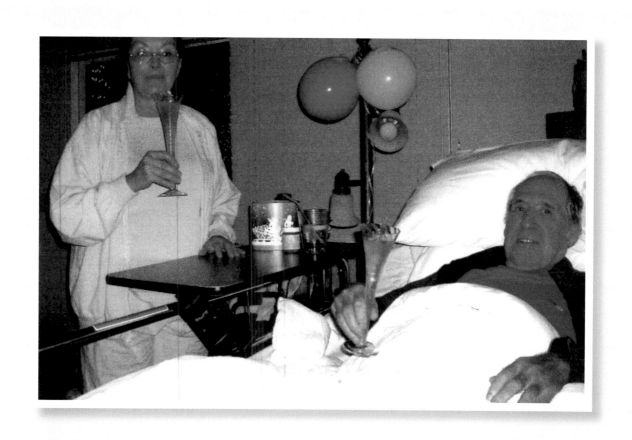

Sandra and My Dad

Sandra was dressed in black the day of my Dad's memorial service. Black blouse and pants were topped with a long, flowing duster coat, which was embroidered along the lower border in an exotic pattern of reds, golds, and oranges. She wore gold sandals and her strawberry blonde hair was done up in chignon. Around her neck, a long, gold chain held a huge amber quartz crystal. She could not have looked more perfect for the occasion.

The memorial service was beautiful. It was a military service since my Dad was a war veteran. I was able to deliver my memories of my Dad out loud without a hitch. Sandra thanked me for representing our family as she and my sister were in no condition to stand up and speak.

Their home was decorated gorgeously for the celebration of life party. Flowers and plants and food and wine were everywhere. A memory-board about my Dad was created by my aunt and cousins. His army jacket was displayed along with many photos, medals, and notes. My cousins kept teasing that my Dad didn't like one particular photo of himself in black, horn-rimmed glasses. It kept falling off the memory-board no matter how many times they glued it in place.

There were so many people, and it really was a party. It was eerie and I kept looking over my shoulder as I sensed my Dad was there. Later in the evening I went out on the patio. A light, warm rain began to fall. It was sad but somehow comforting and I had to think Heaven was crying for us.

Sandra told me later that after everyone had left, the oven buzzer kept going off. She kept turning it off but she somehow knew it was my Dad. The next month she came down to our home for Easter. I didn't want her to be alone. We have a lamp on a table that kept coming on by itself and I had to keep turning it off. It has never done that before or since Sandra visited us that Easter.

Since researching for this book how spirits communicate with our dimension, I am convinced that there are many ways to hear Whispers From Heaven. I think my Dad uses electrical energy to send us messages.

My Dad's cat, Vincent

My Dad was an animal lover. All his life he had dogs and cats. Usually the pets he acquired were animals that had lost their way and found him. Vincent was one of those pets.

Vincenzo, who was a transplant that showed up on my Dad's doorstep one day, was a big, fat Siamese cat. When I say fat, I am not exaggerating. He weighed about 30 pounds, and looked like a pot-bellied pig. Often people were confused to believe it really was a cat. Vincent's belly hung down to the ground and when my Dad first inherited him, he was pathologically shy. Vincent only trusted my Dad. He lived in the closet and would not come out except to eat.

Vincent was black-coated with a little beige around the face and chest. He had beautiful blue eyes. He obviously suffered from a metabolic disorder, but my Dad never took him to the vet. Over the years, Vincent became less shy, even friendly, but never lost the urge to gorge himself. When my Dad died, I volunteered to take Vincent.

I loved Vincent and I think he loved me but he did not get along with my other cat. Vincent wanted to be the boss and eat all the food. He was a terrible car traveler and got sick the whole drive up to Tahoe. I felt sorry for him but I loved him and we tried to get along the best that we could.

One Friday evening I noticed Vincenzo was not eating the way he normally did. I also noticed he wasn't using the litter box. This was obvious because what goes in must come out and A LOT usually came out of Vincent. I thought I would wait until Monday to see if things improved before taking him to the vet.

It was about 12:45 am early Sunday morning when the home alarm sirens starting blaring. We all jumped out of bed from a deep sleep. I grabbed the gun. We were sure we had an intruder. The police came, the alarm company was called, and it was deemed a false alarm. The next morning I started thinking this wasn't a false alarm. Vincent was worse and we took him to the veterinarian that day on an emergency visit. It was determined that Vincent had kidney failure, he was an old cat, and there was no cure. I had to make the difficult decision to put him out of his misery and let him go be with my Dad. My heart broke because I loved

Vincent and he was part of my Dad that I had to let go. The vet put Vincent to sleep without me witnessing the injection. The vet brought Vincent back to me. He looks peaceful and I cried until all his fur was soaking wet.

The repairman from the alarm company came on Monday to determine why the home alarm system erroneously responded early Sunday Morning. He checked all the window and door sensors and the alarm panel. He could not determine that anything was wrong. His diagnosis was, "Maybe you have Poltergeist." "No, I don't have a ghost," I thought. I have a Dad that used electrical energy to tell me to take his fatally ill cat to the vet.

My Mom, Lou

I rolled to the right, saw my cat who sleeps on that side, and moaned to myself when I read the digital clock. It was 2:45 am on Christmas Eve morning as I experienced my insomnia. There was so much to do to finalize Christmas: cooking, cleaning, wrapping. As I went through my mental list of things to do I was looking through the double glass sliders that look out onto the pool from our bedroom. It was a beautiful moonlit night and the pool water was sparkling. Suddenly, to the far end of the slider near the ceiling a light appeared. I thought to myself, "What is that car doing at this time of night, driving at the end of our street, shining its headlights into our house through the front bedroom?" As I listened for the familiar bump-bump in the street that happens when cars drive in front of our house, it never came. But the light was still there and continued to travel across the top of the glass sliders until it reached the end. It became a bright, white orb, then burst and disappeared. "My Mother!!!" I cried in silence.

You see my Mom had been fighting the terminal diagnosis of glioblastoma (malignant brain tumor). It was a tough two years of treatment for my Mom, and it deeply affected our whole family. I remember she held a cross in her hands most of the time. One day she asked me if I could give her the pills to end it all. It broke my heart, but I teased her by saying, "You just want to hurry and go be with Jesus!" She smiled at me as she nodded her head.

After the orb disappeared, I got out of bed, and checked to see if there was a car in our culdesac as I couldn't believe what I just witnessed. I almost called my step-dad. I was baffled but I finally fell back asleep. I was awakened at 7:30 am by the phone ringing. It was my step-dad. He said, "Your Mom went to heaven last night at 2:55 am." All I could say was, "Yes I know daddy, she was here."

A week later we had the memorial party. It was a stunning day in Newport Beach. The sky was sunny, bright blue, and crystal clear. I thought to myself "Lou wouldn't have it any other way." The thought of that light/orb appearing in my bedroom haunted me. I did not discuss it with anyone that day. Only my husband, my son, and my step-dad knew of my story.

Fast forward to two months after the memorial service. I was on social media looking at the photographs my cousin posted from that day. As I perused through them, I stopped at one photo of my step-dad shaking hands with someone at the memorial party. His back was to the camera, but on his right, jacketed arm sat a white orb. I enlarged the photo and was amazed at the clarity. No other photo demonstrated the well-circumscribed orb. Of course Lou would not miss her own goodbye party. I was in shock but felt sure that my Mother came to say goodbye to me the night she passed. And now I had proof in that photo. That was my experience with my first Whisper From Heaven.

After seeing the orb of my Mom in the photo, I wondered if she appeared in other photos of mine. I began to scrutinize the Christmas photos we took the day after she died. Sure enough, there were several photos with the grapefruit-sized orb sitting way up in the dark corner of the photos. I new it could not be the flash of the camera. It was always one white orb with a distinct mottling on the inside. The Easter holiday after my Mom passed we celebrated with the family. Sure enough, as I later looked at the photos, the white orb appeared on stepdad's right arm. That was the last time I ever saw the orb in a photo.

Vickie's Mom

Vickie was very close to her mom and was, of course, devastated when her mother passed away after a critical, brief illness. Vickie was in her forties and felt she was just too young to have lost her mother and best friend. Just a few days after the memorial service, Vickie was reminiscing about her mom while she was sorting through some of the jewelry and belongings her mom had left her. Vickie was upstairs in her bedroom while doing this and suddenly she felt the distinct presence of her mother. She left her bedroom and started to walk downstairs. As she looked down, there in the middle of the stairwell laid a Snickers Candy Bar wrapper. She picked it up while thinking, "Mom you are here with me." You see, Vickie's mother's favorite snack in the world was a Snicker's Bar.

Pam and her Husband

Pam's second marriage was everything her first marriage was not. She felt she had found the love of her life with a wonderful man. When they got married, Pam had a statement engraved inside the gold wedding band her husband, Doug, wore. It said, "To the Love of my Life."

The two of them spent many years together acquiring properties and traveling. They both loved to golf and owned a large home in the desert where they belonged to a private golf club. Doug was having some dental problems and went to have his teeth cleaned. He also suffered from a pre-existing heart condition. The next morning Doug took their dog for a walk, as he usually did. He was about three blocks away from home when he keeled over and died from a massive heart attack. He passed before emergency medical help arrived.

Pam was in shock to say the least. They had planned a trip in their motor home to travel to their property in Montana. Pam's life changed suddenly and unexpectedly and she was trying to come to grips with her new reality. When Pam retrieved Doug's gold wedding band, she was shocked to find that there was no engraving on the inside of the ring. The band was completely shiny gold with no trace of her wedding message. She was perplexed and mentioned it to one of her very spiritual friends who told her, "Doug took your love to heaven with him." To this day Pam feels Doug's presence and knows he helps direct her ongoing attempt to settle her affairs.

Patti and the White Lilies

Patti's mother was starting to feel her age. She loved living alone in her small senior citizen apartment and always filled several vases with white lilies, which was her favorite flower. Shortly, she realized it was not feasible or safe for her to continue on her own. Her son and daughter-in-law were planning a trip to Italy but insisted that she come live with them. The idea was to move her in and then, Patti, her daughter, would look after her until they came home from their trip. Patti's mom was highly concerned about putting a burden on her family. Soon after she moved in with her son and daughter-in-law she became extremely ill and had to be hospitalized. Unfortunately, she died while in the hospital, just a few days after she was admitted. Patti is convinced that she willed herself to death just so she wouldn't be a bother to her son and daughter.

Patti's brother and wife did go to Italy. They had a wonderful time, but what was really curious is that everywhere they traveled they noticed big vases of white lilies. Of course they knew this was their mom's favorite flower and they felt her presence as she blessed their trip. Patti was touched when her brother told her about all the lilies he and his wife saw during their travels. She felt this was her mothers's way of telling them that she was fine.

A few years later Patti's brother passed away in exactly the same hospital room as his mom was in when she died. Patti was at the hospital to say goodbye to her brother. She was curiously surprised that a big vase with white lilies was left outside the door to his hospital room. No one ever could figure out who they were from as there was no card attached to the flower arrangement. But Patti knew exactly who sent them.

Jan and her Dad

Jan was living on the west coast when her elderly father passed away on his farm in middle America. Jan and her sister planned to fly back to arrange for a memorial service. Jan's sister was also bringing her husband and young daughter to pay their final respects. The farm was going to be sold. Since the property was a childhood home to both Jan and her sister, they wanted to visit there and take some photographs. It was spring and the entire land was in bloom with different colored flowers. The front of the house had a big porch, a red barn-style front door, and picture windows which allowed one to look out over the farmland. Jan took a photograph capturing the entire front view of the house along withn several photos of the farmland.

About a month later Jan, her sister, and Jan's niece got together for lunch. Jan wanted to share the photos of their father's memorial service and of his farm. The three of them lingered over the photo of the front view of the farmhouse. Jan's young niece said, " Hey isn't that grandpa in that window?" Jan and her sister looked at each other dumbfounded. Sure enough, there was the face of their dad staring out one of the windows, seemingly directly at them.

Jan cherished that photo, but reports that about a year later her dad's face faded from the window.

Brian and His Daughter, Missy

My friend Brian is what we call a snowbird. He spends half of his time in Olympia, Washington and the other half of the year in the warmer desert climate in Southern California. One of his daughters, Missy, also spends time in both places with her husband and family. The last two years were tough on Missy. Her husband, Don, was ill but, embracing the religion of Christian Science, he never went to a doctor to get diagnosed. The family was staying up north during a rainy winter in their beautiful 3-story home overlooking the ocean. Don was failing rapidly, and required more care just to keep him comfortable. He passed away late one afternoon at his home. It was almost a relief not to have to watch him suffer anymore.

Later that night Missy, her son Steve, and Steve's wife were sitting on the sofa, looking out the second story picture window of their house. The mood was melancholy but the water was spectacular, reflecting the starry night. Suddenly, a bright beam of light seemed to rise up out of the water. The three of them watched as the huge bright orb rose up into the sky, exploded like fireworks, and then slowly disappeared into the night's darkness. The three of them were shocked as they stared out over the water. As they discussed what they had just witnessed, they instinctively knew it was Don's way of saying goodbye to them. All of them said that they were glad they had been together to see Don's final goodbye or they would not have believed it happened.

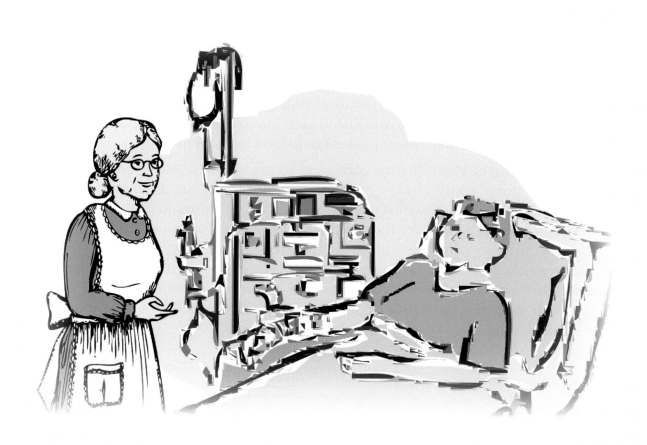

Brian and his Wife, Diane

My dear friend, Brian, not only lost his son-in-law that year, but also lost his wife a few months later. Brian was in his 90's so to say that this life event was a huge disruption in his life and what he considered normal was an understatement. Diane suffered with dementia and crippling loss of body function. Even though she was confused and not aware of reality most of the time, Brian was comforted by her presence. He really did not know what to do with himself after her passing and suffered from depression.

It was just a week or two after Diane died when Brian tells about a dream that he had, although it felt very real. In the dream Brian was in the hospital bed and Diane was at the foot of the bed. She was standing, which she had not been able to do on her own for years. Brian says she looked better than ever, one hundred percent. As he stared at her she said, "Dad, I am OK." Brian thinks of this dream daily and it gives him great comfort. He knows this was Diane's way of letting him know she was alright.

Aunt Fran

Friday's I work in our dental office. This particular day in January 2015 I saw a lady patient that lives in the low-income apartment complex where my Aunt Fran used to live. She knew that Fran and I were very close for many years before we had a falling out in our relationship in 2012. She knew that I was probably unaware that Fran passed away from her bone cancer in November 2014. She thought I probably would want to know that. I cried the minute she told me the news. Our misunderstanding now seemed so trivial.

The rest of the day I felt very sad even though Fran and I had not been in contact for a few years. What is weird is that after being told that Fran had died, I remembered the dream I experienced in November. I call it a dream, but there were no images. It was Fran's voice loud and clear that woke me up. All she said was, "Hi Lynn !!!" I remember thinking, "Oh my gosh, I wonder if she died." A few days later I kept checking the obituaries but never found anything. Yesterday I looked again on the Internet and still could not find any public record of her death. It was strange, but I believe she was letting me know she made it to Heaven. I am glad I finally know she is in peace.

My Sister, Kathy, and the Hummingbird

My Mom, Lou, died December 24, 2012. I already had experienced Whispers from her which I eventually shared with my sister, Kathy. To my surprise, Kathy shared with me how my Mom, communicated with her.

Shortly after my Mom's passing, Kathy told me about a persistent hummginmbird that appeared in her yard. It had a particular coloring that was unique. Apparently this bird shows up at family events. When Jenny, Kathy's daughter, moved into her new home, the hummingbird was spotted flitting around the outside of the house. At the restaurant where Jenny held her baby shower, Ted, Kathy's husband, greeted the hummingbird hovering around the entrance to the venue with a "Hi Lou!" I thought it was a sweet story even though my Whispers from Lou in the form of that mottled orb stopped appearing just a few months after her passing.

One day, a couple of years after Kathy told me that story, I was standing outside under the covered patio on a hot, sunny day in my Palm Desert house. I was in the shade but the brilliant sunlight was a step away. All of a sudden a hummingbird buzzed in front of me at eye level. It hovered for several seconds and I marveled at its beautiful coloring. The bright sun sparkled on its iridescent emerald green head and magenta chest. I don't think I have ever seen a hummingbird with brighter colors. Soon it flew away and I realized that it was my Mom! I ran in the house to call Kathy.

My Friend, Debbie

My best friend and mentor for forty years moved to the Island of Kauai in 1990 as her younger husband was an avid surfer. Tommy and Debbie bought a house there and retired. It was difficult to continue to keep our close friendship on the same level by phone calls and letters. I flew over and stayed in Kauai a couple of times with them but the friendship waned. Communications became fewer and birthday cards went unsent.

It was the summer of 2016 and I was sitting in my Lake Tahoe house one evening when a pressing thought seemed to come to my mind. I felt an overwhelming prompting to call Debbie and Tommy. I had not spoken to them in years and did not have their phone number. I decided to look up their information on my Ipad. Immediately after I typed in their names, Tommy's obituary popped up as the first find in my search. I was in shock. He had just passed away within the last week and a half. Fortunately their home phone number also popped up and I called Debbie right then and there. We reconnected and she shared the details of Tom's death, which were not very pleasant.

The previous month, Debbie had fallen and she had a short stay in the hospital. She and Tom loved to drink heavily, and apparently, Tom drank too much while Debbie was in the hospital. He slipped and fell while in the shower, hit his head and bled to death from the blunt trauma. Someone found him a couple of days later when Debbie became concerned because she was not able to reach him by phone. I was overwhelmed with the information, but was very concerned about how Debbie was holding up, especially since she was just released from the hospital. She told me that her daughter was flying over to stay with her and she invited me to come and visit her also. I did not fly over, but we began to reconnect by long phone conversations every few days.

It was Thanksgiving time. Debbie called me and told me she was diagnosed with cirrhosis of the liver and didn't have much longer to live. I cried my eyes out, telling her it wasn't fair as we were just renewing our friendship. She said she was in peace about it, and all her affairs were in order. The doctor gave her medication and told her when she got tired of it all, just stop taking the meds. She would soon enter a coma and would die within three days. I asked her what she was doing for Thanksgiving. She told me her son and daughter were with her and she was getting takeout from her favorite French restaurant and she was going to have a big glass of wine.

I didn't speak to Debbie except one more time before Christmas as she was becoming weaker. I was busy creating a Tahoe Christmas for my son and husband. I planned to call Debbie the day after Christmas. It was the morning of December 26 and I was awakened by a strange dream. In my dream I saw a large shield that had five golden circles looped together, sort of like the Olympic Rings. Below in big, bold, capital letters was Debbie's name. I immediately got up and drew a picture of what I saw in my dream. I called Debbie but did not get an answer so I called my step-mom who was in touch with Debbie's daughter. She told me Debbie had passed away on December 16. I was shocked that no one informed me but I was curious about my dream. When I looked at the image I drew, the shield looked more like a tombstone. I searched on the internet what 5 interlocking gold rings meant. The answer: ETERNITY. Thank you Debbie for that Whisper From Heaven.

Danielle and the Baseball

My friend Danielle came to stay with me in Tahoe. We shopped, dined, played golf, and laughed until we cried. The night before she was to fly out she received a text from her daughter that her dad (Danielle's ex- husband, Ted) had died. He had been ill for awhile so it was not a shock..... or was it? Danielle was visibly upset when she read the text and began to cry. Even though she had not seen her ex-husband for many years, she was shaken by the news. As she put it, an era and milestone of a part of her life had now ended.

I decided to take her out to dinner to one of my favorite restaurants. While we were getting ready, I said a small prayer to Ted. I said that even though I had never met him, I know that he held an important place in Danielle's life. I asked if he would please give Danielle a sign that he was OK. I did not disclose to Danielle that I had said this prayer. We enjoyed a lovely dinner and it was dusk when we left the restaurant.

A sliver of Luna floated above Mt. Rose with a bright Venus by her side. The mountains were lit up by the backdrop of a purple sky. We stepped off the curb as we walked towards my car. Suddenly, I looked down and spotted something white and round lying on the ground right in front of us. At first I thought someone had dropped a muffin. "What is that?" I asked. Danielle bent over and picked up a brand new professional baseball. Shivers went up my spine as I asked her, "Did Ted like baseball?" She stopped and looked at me with astonishment as she told me that Ted loved baseball and he had played in the minor leagues. Ted actually taught their grandson how to play and now he was playing on a school team. I confessed to Danielle the prayer I had said to Ted earlier that evening. I told her that the baseball we had found in our path was a Whisper From Heaven as Ted wanted to let Danielle know he was OK.

About the Author

Lynn McKendry was born and raised in Southern California. She practiced dental hygiene for 35 years and taught as assistant professor at Loma Linda University School of Dentistry for thirteen years. She holds two master degrees and a doctoral degree. She and her husband managed and practiced dentistry in several locations, including a charitable dental clinic which delivered dentistry to low-income senior citizens. Lynn wrote two children's books about "Jerry the Bunny" which were inspired by her son. Now retired, Lynn wrote her first nonfiction book "Whispers From Heaven" after experiencing messages from loved ones that had passed. As she shared these stories with family and friends, more stories emerged and are documented in her book. Lynn spends time between Lake Tahoe and Palm Desert. She enjoys boating, snow skiing, golf, and cooking.

Printed in the United States
By Bookmasters